WAYWARD

WAYWARD

poems

✖

Katharine Coles

🐦 Red Hen Press | *Pasadena, CA*

Library of Congress Cataloging-in-Publication Data

Names: Coles, Katharine, author.
Title: Wayward : poems / Katharine Coles.
Description: First edition. | Pasadena, CA : Red Hen Press, 2019.
Identifiers: LCCN 2018042732| ISBN 9781597098953 | ISBN 1597098957
Classification: LCC PS3553.O47455 A6 2019 | DDC 811/.6—dc23
LC record available at https://lccn.loc.gov/2018042732

The National Endowment for the Arts, the Los Angeles County Arts Commission, the Ahmanson Foundation, the Dwight Stuart Youth Fund, the Max Factor Family Foundation, the Pasadena Tournament of Roses Foundation, the Pasadena Arts & Culture Commission and the City of Pasadena Cultural Affairs Division, the City of Los Angeles Department of Cultural Affairs, the Audrey & Sydney Irmas Charitable Foundation, the Kinder Morgan Foundation, the Meta & George Rosenberg Foundation, the Allergan Foundation, and the Riordan Foundation partially support Red Hen Press.

First Edition
Published by Red Hen Press
www.redhen.org

ACKNOWLEDGMENTS

Ascent: "Ice Age," "On Sappho," "Question of the Soul"; *Axon*: "Thirst," "Narrative," "Lunar Eclipse," "Hawk"; *Crazyhorse*: "Self-Portrait with Nightfall," "How We Sing," "Cento with Typo, from a Blog by Errol Morris"; *DIAGRAM*: "Landscape with Angel," "New Clothes," "Equinox"; *Epiphany*: "Wayward" (as "Way/ward"); *Gargoyle*: "Self-Portrait Up in the Air," "Canis Latrans"; *The Georgia Review*: "The New Day"; *Hudson Review*: "Misreading"; *Image*: "Annunciation," "Bewilder"; *The Journal*: "Landscape with Alchemist"; *Mudlark*: "Hive," "Self-Portrait from a Negative," "Taste of a Wound Not Healing," "Submersible," "Longevity"; *North Dakota Review*: "The Archimedes Palimpsest"; *Poetry*: "From the Middle," "From Space," "Kept in Mind," "The Same Old Riddle"; *Seneca Review*: "New Year Cento on Infinity and Mortality"; *Terrain*: "The Things We Observe in the Universe Are Not the Important Things," "Shell," "Landscape with Bodies"; *Weber*: "Summer Has No Day," "Hideout," "Canis Veritatem Contemplator," "In Our Twenty-fifth Summer," "Away."

Twenty-five of these poems were included in *Bewilder,* a chapbook published in fall 2015 by Axon/The International Poetry Studies Institute at the University of Canberra, Australia. "Canis Sollicitor," "Landscape with Bronzes and Little Rooms," "Once," "In Store," "Oldest Known Love Poem," "Canus Nigrem," "August," "Rip Tide," "Knowing," and "In the Garden" had their first publication in that volume.

"Broken Renga" was commissioned for and forms a link in *The World Keeps Turning to Light: a Renga by the State Poets Laureate of America.*

Many of these poems were written and some were published as part of a collaborative conversation with visual artist Maureen O'Hara Ure for an artist's book, *Stranger and Stranger,* commissioned by the Red Butte Press at the University of Utah.

CONTENTS

∞

WAYWARD

∞

HOW WE SING

With our leg bones. With alphabets
And lambkins. With bat-wings

Hung out to dry. With the birds.
With our heads on our sleeves. From

The lion's throat, in stitches. Riding
The backs of dragons. Bohemian,

Spare-pantried, squeezing our boxes,
Penises wagging, breasts akimbo, mouthing

Feet, hearts in our hands, whistles
Whetted. Bare faced. Captive. In time.

CANIS SOLLICITOR

Make room for doubt. Dig
And roll in the cool hollow

And snooze. Dig some more. Find
A bone you buried last year

Or before then forgot. Believe
You have no past or future, no

Idea. Chew and gnaw and worry
What if you're the hard

Core of everything. What might
Be wrong, hold together.

LANDSCAPE WITH ANGEL

What does it need with wings? It lofts
Over soft hills and furrows with no apparent
Energy or effort, feathers and frock
And hairdo all unfluttered. Urgency

Expresses itself only through the horizontal
Body, or would if this messenger didn't
Look stiff as a board surfing the air. While
We're at it, why does it wear clothes? No small

Human embellishments hide among the drapes,
No secret conceals itself in cunning folds.
(If it's earth's, not heaven's, the landscape

Lies always under night, dotted with lights
Which might be tended fires and might be wild,
On the edge of hope, the edge of blow-up.)

WAYWARD

Will sally for any direction you name,
Or not. After, back, in, too,

Out to follow. Down
Like a dog or some hero

Sunk into his own private
Guided tour of hell. Some of us,

Cowed, go home and weave.
Others take to sea to find

How many animal shapes
Contain them. I might have

A horn on my nose or more
Arms than I can tell what

To do, as many brains, eyes
In my palms or odd

Numbers of hearts
Unbiddable. Good

Heaven, do unto
Or just feed them—I'd rather

Think what greens
Mean in numbers or how

A sky's dazzle blinds
And blisses. East, west: no way

To know, is the thing, what
To count, how far to go.

THE ARCHIMEDES PALIMPSEST

Not erased.   Equations painted
Over.   *Curious mathematics.*   *A leaf*

A spiral   *a ghost* fluttering
The edge of vision, *a style of inquiry*   *all there is*

To find out.   So
Give it up: evangelists here live in

Color, mouths popped around
(*Leaves   disappear* in flight)

New truth.   Beneath, behind,
A set of pieces can be

Arranged in the form of a square.   What did
Archimedes draw?   *Straight lines*

Off-kilter   floating bodies
(Old-time preachers again)   *more like*

Examples than proofs   *turn instead to*
A radical idealization. If time is not a river

Maybe one mind absorbs
Into another then bleeds out *accumulated*

Catastrophes, not every advance
Improvement. The past

As it will be, *hints*
And layers recoverable:

Interpreted   the diagram shows
Not known.

ANNUNCIATION

What matters is what occurs occurs
Between them, not to them. It's only that
The angel doesn't matter, nor the virgin.
A blade of light scissors the air

Between them. To them it's only that:
A glancing blow, or a kind of cleaving,
A blade of light. Scissor the air
Wide open, then it happens:

A glance, a blow, error a kind of cleaving—
Of? Or to? So something else can enter.
Open wide then. It happens
Those two forget themselves, not knowing—

What? or who?—so something else can enter
And, in entering, replace them.
We can't forget ourselves. Knowing
Carelessness has brought us to the point

Where in entering we replace them.
The angel doesn't matter, nor the virgin.
Carelessness has brought us to the point.
What is matters. What occurs, occurs.

THE NEW DAY

Enters in the heroic mode, feathered
And helmeted, muscle-bound

For glory, smelling of scorch. Raise
That sword a little higher

If you can lift it and buckle your straps
Tight. *Insert fanfare.* Nobody still

Gets to ride the train all afternoon
Dozing. Scotch that clickety-clack, the sudden

Dark plunge. In the underworld nobody gets to be
Just a body any more, ripe, a little bloody,

And needing its toenails clipped. Me, poor
Me, I'm steeping in juices, greased

And gristled. In the past I've been pretty
Enough, though, to make up for anything.

NEW CLOTHES

A coat of softest skin. The emperor
Admiring his ensemble in the mirror
Admires himself. His error:

It's not his skin. He's blinded by finery
Fillips at scrotum and throat, has an awry
Relationship to the material, airy

As chiffon and lace, as insouciance is
And insouciant gesture, a séance's
Whisper thrilling his spine. Once is

Enough, or once was: silk delicious,
Velvet's stroke dark and luscious
At nape. Now, his mind says, *Shush*—

Understanding can't hold you together.
Only the sack of skin can gather
Organ and bone in. What gathers skin? Other

To every other. To impulse
His heart beats *yes*, pulse
An ornament at his wrist. Nothing else

To do now but surrender
Desire to desire. What desire renders?
He'll be fine if he stays indoors.

SUBMERSIBLE

Little man at the window keeps saying
What's your system. He has
Buttons to push and levers in red
Rubber sleeves; looking out

Over the dash he wants to think
I'm deep, wants to steer
Something forth, and all
That's on my mind is that pair

Of blue patent creepers, their precisely
Pointed toes. It's always been
This way, the world open-faced
And full of shoes and submarines

Ready to dive, me putting
Nose clips on, ready to follow.

THE SAME OLD RIDDLE

We keep trying to kill it, split it, hack
It to itsy bits. We suspend it
On the wall where we can see it
Passing. We hang it around our necks

Or wrists, laying pulse next to
Pulse as if each might like
Company. Ba-bump, etc. Rising
And setting has everything to do

With it. In the afternoon we feel so
Lazy we try not to close our eyes
And jerk awake, wondering what has
Passed, and where did we go

During that suspended hour,
And could anything keep us here.

KNOWING

And if we grieve in anticipation, will we
Take the edge off or only bring grief

Down? How many long
Summer days spent mourning summer

Passing. Feeling the shadow
Fall, trying to remember who once said

The saddest song is the sparrow's. For so long
We've tried to name its note

High and urgent, no sadder than any song
That starts and stutters. The sparrow fluffs his wings

And tries the air again. What
We can't bear. Trying. Going wrong.

NEW YEAR CENTO ON
INFINITY AND MORTALITY

There are the infinities of the everyday,
Pale green and vaguely ruffled, like calcified doilies,

Like the weather, the economy and human stupidity.
Most people barely notice them.
They deteriorate with the passage of time.

Think of the world as being infinitely divisible.
Is immortality biologically possible?

If the universe is infinite the answer has to be yes.
Time can be twisted. The finite is nested
Within the infinite. Death as we know it rests

On an animal-centered idea of individuality.
The ancient Greeks abhorred the very notion of it.

It can be quite subtle and quite dangerous.
It may be an infinite bubble bath, which grows
To be as heavy as a blue whale. A lichen

May live forever, a biologist will not. *That's mortality.*
There are flat infinities, hunchback infinities,

Hyperboloid infinities. *You will get duplicates.* In short,
Your doppelgängers may be out there. Some
Are tailored for mathematics, some for cosmology,

Others for theology. They hardly lead a carefree life:
"The infinite" topped the column of bad traits

Like femininity. *Those are the organisms that broke*
All the rules. Some infinities are bigger than others.
A bus can still run over them. Death

Is not everything. No one has ever proved that,
Though, or even collected much data.

RIP TIDE

Another drowning. A brother
Goes under, rises, keeps again

Vanishing while we try to wade
The current then run side-to-side looking

Maybe for a boat before we fall
Still, arms at our sides, hands

Helpless as fish. Can't he hear us calling
From our safe shore? Who knew the future

Would be so deep and swift. We cannot reach him
And there's some surface

He cannot breach. It turns
And glints at us in turning. A wave

Could take him, any curl or ripple could
Knock him under. And does, and does.

IN STORE

Grown too large, his brain
Untethered itself and flew. He folded

His thoughts down neatly
And shut the drawer. Who knew

When he would ever need them
And who knows what they do, pressed

Cheek-to-cheek in the dark
Holding tight, trying not to breathe.

TASTE OF A WOUND
NOT HEALING

Without licking
A finger, without

Touching a thing. It is
Already inside, lying

Its long body along
The tongue. Stretch

And purr. What luxury,
Nothing left to do.

INTERIOR

Maybe the mummy lost his heart
When it was alive, to art

Or a hand's press soft
Before it tightened, distraught.

Or he was always heartless.
On screen, regardless,

We can see he's fallen
To pieces, chamber collapsed on

Itself or
Vanished, a door

Opening on air. Perhaps
He's missing it and perhaps

Not. What can a poor mummy do
Without? The matter becomes

Absence. He's lost something
Big, we know, the thing

Without which, et cetera, whatever
It may have been, or where.

THIRST

Her mother fasted and vanished
As will mine. *A form of self-*

Mummification, my grandmother
Lying as I last saw her, dried to sinew, flesh

Bruised with anger that would not stop
Marking her from inside. *Many waters cannot*

Quench love. Will, then. *It cannot be accomplished*
Impulsively. Before she began, she broke

Her hip, or hip
Broke under her

Small weight. Self losing
Itself falls into the hands of others

Meaning well. Eschew determinedly. Passing
Hunger, give up coffee. Last, surrender

The highball taken every evening
For seventy years. *Love is better*

Than wine, though even alone,
She put on lipstick. Water-starved, entered

Her swoon. *For I am*
Sick in love. Get one thing

Right: wet lips and tongue, do not
Swallow. *It would be a personal assault*

For someone to force water. Still, *I would*
Cause thee to drink of the juice

Of my pomegranate. What gets transmitted,
In what order. In truth I already sense

A bit of headache, cramp
Coming on. *All ages may feel sudden*

Head rushes, dizziness. The body swings
A hundred windows wide to blow in

Cold delirium. Brace. Self, I could be
Flooded, scoured by air. *Ravished*

My heart. Given
Lightness imagine flight.

EMPTY

First zero is absent is un-
Known then becomes

Knot imagined, brought
To mind and so

Being. Take a body,
Present. Arms

Breast belly brain going
Slack then passing

Almost without notice, until
Nothing must remain

Somewhere. Imagine
Sizes of nothing: room-

Ful, coffin, universe blowing
The mind its

Eye largest. All absolute
Nothing, mere

Thimble her fingertip
Used to rest though she

Was anything but old-
Fashioned, knowing

More about the body than I
Can yet imagine. Taste

Illness bitter-
Sweet on the skin

Unto death, beating
All. Nothing

She has become grows not
Bigger nor smaller. Most

Will never see that
Old comet baboom-

Erang by, shedding
Ice into the cold.

BREATH

And a word vanishes off
The lips becoming

Secret. Where will

What it means go and where
Be found. Probably I won't

Know it lands on my tongue

Saying *snowflake, salt,*
Gravel. Like me, probably

Lost to itself.

ON SAPPHO

So time reduces
To essence. We persist, scrap

And word. For example,
A tatter of papyrus, one

Word remaining. I sit
Quiet in my chair but my heart moves

Swift as a sparrow in flight. I am
Moon or green grass, beloved skin

Erased, craving sweet apples
And already sated. If this is

What time leaves—
Bliss, heartbreak, heartbeat,

Dapple of morning sun—
Isn't it heaven.

WHY WE ALWAYS FUCK BEFORE A FUNERAL

Someone has to get
This party going.

Because the universe has no pulse
We check each other's,

Pity, pity, pity, because *knock knock*
Who's there and what

The fuck is this,
A funeral?

ANOTHER BEAST

Winged like us. Part divine, part
Divination. Pleasure is in

Knowing, not knowing. Who
Never could say. Who can't guess

What god might be thinking, any
God at any moment, or how

A deity might tell us what
It thinks. Who keeps finding

Lint in her bathrobe pockets and little
Sweets that have lost their wrappers.

Oh, sweet. Oh, loss. God knows
Where anything goes.

JUST A THOUGHT

If I could see a tree branch
Meandering. Climb into it, take
Its limbs in hand, tender leaves
Dancing while I perch

And settle, holding tight, hoping
Wind won't rise or earth
Shake me down or fire
flock then fly, chittering

Crown to crown. If it fell
Would I be there to hear? Let's
Go back. Lovely, leafing there,
Loafing in it, mouth full

And munching, hands also
Full, and open, shattered.

∞

just a thought

if I could **see** a tree branch
meandering. Climb into it, take
its limbs in hand, tender **leaves**
dancing while I perch

and settle, holding tight, hoping
wind won't rise or earth
shake me down **or** fire
flock then **fly**, chittering

                    narrative

                                                    where **am I**
                    but lost in a thicket of details, **not** knowing why

                        the red shoe lies on the carpet, its tongue
                        lolling out, or whose back is vanishing

                        out the side door. *is anyone home,* I call
                        into **an empty room**. *is anyone ever coming back?*

NARRATIVE

Outside my window
Leaves cling to their branches, all yellow's

Colors, refusing to fly until they do. Where am I
But lost in a thicket of details, not knowing why

The red shoe lies on the carpet, its tongue
Lolling out, or whose back is vanishing

Out the side door. *Is anyone home*, I call
Into an empty room. *Are you coming back?*

FROM THE MIDDLE

How much of everything is pure
Getting ready. Dressing, pushing the button
Asquint through its machined furl
Only to unbutton, the eyes-open moment

Revealed. Ask any animal: nudity isn't
The same as nakedness. Once you've seen
A dangling, you can't unsee it, and
From that anything might ensue.

There's the rub. Taking the long view
You could say the future is romantic
I suppose. Also something you
Could never do without, though its bric-

a-brac is purely theoretical, until
It's arranged. Or not. Then, a miracle?

MISREADING

On (probably) misunderstanding an account of
how to translate verbs in the Hebrew Bible

"Time is the mind of the stars," one critic says
Plutarch said Pythagoras said, in his
Own words. "We are alone in a universe,"
The critic also said, but this was the eighties

And he may be right even now if we confess
The multiplicity of universes, all those
Possible other dwellings in which we may be
Alone. But probably not. Say in *this*

Universe desire imbeds itself in the verb,
Which embodies therefore every form
Of wanting. Say the verb commands you
Or merely permits; say it passes moodiness

Clause to clause, endlessly on time
Even when it seems to change its mind.

CENTO WITH TYPO, FROM
A BLOG BY ERROL MORRIS

We know there is a *real world*. It is not *in us*.
The image and the name of the object encounter each other.

It doesn't matter what's in our heads
But we will pass over this for the time being.

Our brains are just big lumps of electric jelly,
Also splotches of ink on a page.

The theory of a mistake has obtained widely.
The trunk in the attic clearly involves something else—

It is a looking glass in which you see yourselves.
Resemblance is not reference nor is it denotation.

Try to recover something about the world.
There are Newtonian "explanations"

For the precession of the perihelion of Mercury.
It is not in our brains, it is in the world

People don't suddenly become other people.
I have constructed a time machine and I go back,

An animal which must feed upon grass. Resemblance
Is not reference, nor is it detonation.

BEWILDER

He made the Leviathan for the sport of it,
The lord of my childhood. Her fluke

The size of two sleek rowboats
For lifting and drawing down

Knifelike into the water
Or for slapping—so many gestures

A fluke or fin can make with or
Without ruin. I remember

A whale rolling sideways
Just—it appeared—so I could see her

Waving or flirting, her eye deeply
Winking at my eye, no more

Human for that. Can't
Even say she was real beyond

The tide of my imagining or I
Beyond hers, so completely out

Of scale were we, so soundly
Did she sink and finally not

Come up. The lord of my childhood
Made her to flirt and nurse, to sing

But not to me, for
Enchantment and for love. Believing

I am not superstitious, I make
Her like any muse

To bewilder me, to say
As the wave curls overhead cast

Loose, be charmed, be lost, for
Godsake remember be wild.

LANDSCAPE WITH ALCHEMIST

A kind of ingenious nonsense,

Metals and what you made of them required
Exquisite imagination: copper

And silver twisting roots underground, as if

They could bear fruit; silver and mercury
Vegetating in the beaker, branching elegant dendrites

Over the glass; or silica and iron rising to break

Crimson blooms open. A kind of greenhouse. Treasure
Chamber, hoard. Or simple chemistry,

What my brothers mixed up with their white-cased sets

Hinged open centuries later onto what was for you
The knowable unknown, for them the repeatable

Knowing what they saw would turn

Beautiful but not immortal. Why do I keep
Looking behind? You might have imagined

Our century, too, all your beautiful rules

Waiting to be broken. Remember those bottles
And beakers so orderly arrayed, before

Experiment, reaction, explosion.

SELF-PORTRAIT FROM A NEGATIVE

I am not something inside me. I do not
Need to turn inside-
Out to get at the heart of things, to what

I wear on my sleeve breaking
And breaking on itself, beating
That same dead horse. How many times

A lifetime will I be not
My brain flipping out. Could I be
The sense of something pressing

Fingertips, salt on my tongue. A flash,
Rumors I believe, so many
Tickles, a rumbling. My mind

Is played—breeze over a field, a million
Separate blades of grass moving
One body, unison.

FROM SPACE

You are smaller than I remember
And so is the house, set downhill
Afloat in a sea of scrub oak. From up here
It's an ordinary box with gravel

Spread over its lid, weighting it, but
Inside it's full of shadows and sky.
Clouds pull themselves over dry
Grass, which, if I'm not mistaken, will erupt

Any minute in flame. Only
A spark, a sunbeam focused. From up
Here, enjoying the view, I can finally
Take you in. Will you wave back? I keep

Slingshotting around. There's gravity
For you, but all I ever wanted was to fly.

SENSIBLE

How sound exists only
In the brain. In the eye,

Appearance of color, gorgeous
Blue unfolding of sky a matter of

Which rods you have, makes you
Wonder what you're missing. Sense

As structure, depending
Only on itself. What is in here,

I keep having to ask, if ever
I want to know.

SELF-PORTRAIT UP IN THE AIR

I never knew fruit could be room specific, apple
For kitchen, mango for bedroom or bath. So many

Things I've missed or was never told, and where
Does any of it leave me. I could be

Fooled by any cross-dressing harrier, fluffing
Sexy plumes, flying under the radar, hearing

Leisure has nothing to do with lying
Down. What I don't know could

_____ me to the moon. I let my eyes owl out
And peer into the dark. How

Deep could it go? Don't say my eyes
Are bigger than my brain, bluer, buggier, full of outside

Information. Say
I am wayward, fully tricked out. I'm awatch.

DOES THE EARTH MOVE

The evidence: days so still
Light solidifies. Days swept with wind
Flying so fast they buzz

Your whole body. When you step
The ground meets you
Right where you want it, solid

And rising. Or the ground opens
Into quicksand, a sinkhole, earthquake
Or who knows what will

Take you. I will, as long
As you'll let me. As far as the end
If it comes. Beyond if I can.

In for a dime,

My mother said, *in for a lifetime of dollars*:
The prizewinner returns for annual
Letters of praise; the child who opens

Her mouth for the nipple and spoon
Will extend her hand for the keys
Or jimmy the gates. Except my mother

Never said it, I did. Eighty-five, she turns
Over the family silver, her uncle's fallen-
Apart four-string banjo nobody can tune,
Her grandmother's diamond pin, making me

Take as she fails and I let her give
Me no choice, knowing from me she wants
Only patience and time, what she keeps on
Needing and I keep running short of.

DENIAL

Today he declines
Everything but kisses,
Refuses to lie down
And refuses to get up.

Nothing but my kiss
Recovers his attention,
Will persuade him to stand up
And begin his painful walk.

To get his attention
I bring him old photos,
Begin the long walk
Into a captive past.

I show him the photos
To test our memories,
What past we've captured
And can bring to mind:

A picture of me, perhaps,
At my long-since wedding;
His own reminded self
Standing beside my mother

Before their long-held vows.
A lifetime ago—mine—

Since he stood beside her
Straight-backed, full of nerves:

A life I'm almost
Lost to. He recovers,
Stands up, keeps his nerve.
Because his mind is going,

I recover what he's lost.
He refuses to lie down,
Because. I think he's going.
Today, he declines.

ONCE

I could have told you. Then, I would have
Had to. Long ago, and there were

Too many roses, little black beetles
Masticating the leaves. The hidden place gives

Its flower perfume. I wish I'd kept
A secret from you. I wish you knew it.

THE QUESTION OF THE SOUL

Birdsong. Oboe's
Breath. Wind in the eaves, voice

Of the sparrow someone says
Is five notes I can't count. Does

The mind breathe or
My lungs. Throb or

Heart, awash. Electric,
Stricken, it casts

Itself at the air. Beats
And will not

Fly. Wherever might
It go? Dreaming mind caught

Again in the leaves.
Don't look down, I know, keep

Paddling, feeling
Pulse as glee. Moonlight too

Is all the moon's
Sleight of hand, its sly

Deception. A window. Eye
Falls on me.

IN OUR TWENTY-FIFTH SUMMER

The crickets were early. Cicadas

Suddenly click in the trees, ten

Thousand panicked clocks reminding us

It's been—thirteen years

Already? Seventeen? I never

Do remember and who can

Think in such racket, tick tick tick,

Tock tock, extravaganza

Of sex and biting off more

Than can be chewed. So begins

Another cycle, another, each

Anniversary coming to make

Its own mark. What year

Did I decide he didn't need

To understand me? As if we could

Arrive even periodically at

Such knowledge, could ever

Say this, then this, then this

And be proved right.

LONGEVITY

In a world full of poison you survived
The copperhead you carried into
Your mother's kitchen whipping

Its tail while she screamed. Your father
Beheaded it with a shovel on the linoleum
Then beat you blue. That was just

The first. Later came water moccasins,
Rattlers, asp at breast
And scorpion at the heel, black widow

Hiding in the laundry minding
Her own bloody hourglass until your hand
Reached in: the world provided

No such end but left you after
All that for me and for me counting down
Bite by bite what eats you.

CARNAL

Who can pluck its hairs from head
Who can play at its cool heart
In whose arms will it forget
And forgetting fall apart

Will it curl around its dream
With another's breath beside
Will it curl around its sleep
Or show me what its sleeping hides

And in the night will turn again
And in turn expose its throat
Fragile pulse beneath the skin
I crave and will never know

KEPT IN MIND

Hildegard believed
A woman's brain drew

Heat to itself, drew seed
From a man all the way up

The spine's long stair
The stake bracing the spine

Licking all the way orange,
Red, blue—shut it—

And why not? My brain has been
Hungry all this time.

THE OLDEST KNOWN LOVE POEM

Is carved on a sheet of marble
And lives in a museum in Istanbul.

Was whispered into an ear
Sometime during the ice age. Still

Mutters itself over swells
And whorls as long as an ocean,

Pink and gleaming, a throat laid open
Too slick to resist. Was scratched

On someone's belly with a stick.
My belly bleeding now

A little, only a little raw. Love,
Of course, your stick.

NO END TO HAPPINESS,

No end to woe. No way to know
Which weighs more. Today
Bliss carries my small boat

Turning, oars lost already
Miles upstream. Bliss
A word we're barely allowed
These days to use. Now

The boat spins, sky flashes
Blue through leaves where
A pirol lofts its song, pure
Gold on the ear. The air

A faint trembling. Downstream
Could be anywhere.

STRANGER AND STRANGER

All love is odd. Never again
From a distance shall I see you
Unless we are torn
Asunder. What could rend you

Now from me, apart from final
Rendering? Don't growl
At me. Dogbody, I'm not your
Monstrosity—only a simple

Furnishing of life, no stranger
Than the hound lazing at your feet,
Inhabiting the persistent fact
Of flesh, passing weird. Linger

With me here, in twilight's gruff
Boredom. Don't nod off.

EITHER THEY WERE HUMAN

Or they were not. Like us,
They wanted shelter. Like us,
They painted their walls, surrounding
Inside with outside once they had time, once

They wanted shelter, like us,
To be more than what it was,
Outside-in. Once, we had time; once
We too painted a wall

To be more than what it was,
With human figures and figures of beasts.
We too painted a wall
As if we could bring stone to life

With figures of humans. The figures of beasts—
Remember how they danced
As if they could bring stone to life.
There in the flickering light

Remember how we danced,
Among deer light as dreams, vivid
And flickering there in the light.
Big cats wearing spots stalked mammoth

And dream-light deer, so vivid
In our dreams they kept trading places
With big cats wearing spots, stalking mammoth
Then one another

Into our dreams. They kept trading places.
They painted their walls, surrounding
One, then the other.
They were not like us.

CANEM NIGRUM

At the door, licks
Or checks its teeth. Closes

Eyes and gnaws *just*
Where you think

Your heart is. Dogs you, head
Lowered at heel, hungry

As, pulling
The leash. Slips

Light to shadow then
Brings shadow back,

Remember, and lays it down
Every corner, along

Folds and wrinkles,
The coats in the closet,

The sheets. Faithful, *always*
Only yours. Remember

The clearing, no locks
Or keys, woods

Pressing in. How you lit
A fire to eat the dark

And made yourself
Inviting. What line

Separates your moony
Mind and the world

You can feel, until
A lean shadow crosses,

Head lowered, set down
Sure-handed, in ink.

ICE AGE

The aurochs spins in firelight *suspended*
On the tent. Appears to run, *remarkable*

Shadows, foolery already
Leaping. Carved from bone: a map,

A tool for scraping snow, river, a blizzard,
A fish. What *is a wonder of nature?* A leaf,

A weapon, a lion-man 40,000 years ago
Carved from the bone of a mammoth. Still *the arrival*

And departure of birds. Two reindeer
(16,000 years, 20,000) swimming or a male

Nosing under a female's tail, like me riveted
In time. *The wooly rhino is an extinct species.* Still

Dressed for cold though outside
Trees are in bud, gauzed with green. Already, see,

Makers swoon, in thrall to themselves
Making. *When they stand up on their back legs*

Bears resemble humans. This man's head
Turns like a doll's. This one was in pain, riven

By time. *River pebbles minimally altered to accentuate*
Their female features. Mouth open, is she

Calling or screaming? *Are these real women*
Or imaginary beings? Their brains, the gloss tells us,

Were like ours. An argument made
Or had. Is the brain the mind? I

Forget. In wild speculation, I always say
It slipped my mind. I mean, reality.

∞

ice age

the aurochs spins in firelight *suspended*
on the tent. appears to run, *remarkable*

shadows, foolery already
leaping. carved from bone: a map,

a tool for scraping snow, river, a blizzard,
a fish. what **is a wonder** *of nature?* a leaf,

a weapon, a lion-man 40,000 years ago
carved from the bone of a mammoth. still *the arrival*

and departure of birds. two reindeer
(16,000 years, 20,000) swimming or a male

nosing under a female's tail, **like me riveted**
in time. *the wooly rhino is an extinct species.* still

dressed for cold though outside
trees are in bud, gauzed with green. already, see,

makers swoon, **in thrall** to themselves

self-portrait **with nightfall**

and all **you find** gazing out from where you are is light

blazing the house across the way, where you imagine
neighbors you haven't met baking potatoes

or settling down in front of the tv, looking to fill

another long **vacancy**. you know that **light**
catching the grass almost as far as the sidewalk

will never reach you. see? out back, across the ravine,

a campfire burns at eye level, **suspended**. have you
forgotten where the ground is? before the flames flicker

shadows with nowhere else to go. september, nights begin

shivering, the first breath from the north. **where** will those
ghosts sleep when the snow flies? and where **will you be**

when the field has **already erased** itself?

SELF-PORTRAIT WITH NIGHTFALL

Say you were born with a congenital absence, one

You can see, a space you should have
A digit or a limb to flutter and wave at

The world, hang out on the air—or you're missing

Something invisible, a chemical in the brain that tells you
Smile now, a piece of gristle your heart needs

To beat in synchrony. Mutter all you want: in this

You are different from nobody, even in your feeling
Alone at night when darkness brings itself down

And all you find gazing out from where you are is light

Blazing the house across the way, where you imagine
Neighbors you haven't met baking potatoes

Or settling down in front of the TV, looking to fill

Another long vacancy. You know that light
Catching the grass almost as far as the sidewalk

Will never reach you. See? Out back, across the ravine,

A campfire burns at eye level, suspended. Have you
Forgotten where the ground is? Before the flames flicker

Shadows with nowhere else to go. September, nights begin

Shivering, the first breath from the north. Where will those
Ghosts sleep when the snow flies? And where will you be

When the field has already erased itself?

THE THINGS WE OBSERVE IN THE UNIVERSE
ARE NOT THE IMPORTANT THINGS

Not deaths of stars, spectacular, but darknesses
Thickened between them, any invisible

Pull. Blood surging, thought ticking over
A dog's brain the moment she decides I am

Dangerous or not, biteful or tender making
A smell or gesture only the dog can read. Her brain

Composes knowledge a fish walked
Out onto shore so long ago neither the dog

Nor I remembers. We could have come out
Different. If I were to count up all we hold

In common, what might I call her? Relative. Fish
And fowl. *Swish, swish.* I hold my hands palm

Down and the tail waves. *Patience.* No
More than deepening space between flashes of light,

Reliable or erratic, heart and soul. *Gravy.* My hands
Accept the lash of tongue. Tasting, to be sure.

CANIS VERITATEM
CONTEMPLATOR

Pursue the usual avenues—genetic
Testing or Myers-Briggs
Or plain old talky
Talky talky, resort
To dream, theory, calculations
Written on a napkin
In some beer hall. So
I'm not a dog as such. Results
Come in and someone
Reads them to us, we all
Sniff each other's butts, still
Nothing's settled. The universe
Is built to deliver answers
One at a time, not tell us
What they mean. Or
Where would we be.

MARRIAGE

It may go wrong. For it
Then in a measured way, a zealot
Tempered by watching, I'm softened
Under reality's hard press,

The one-said-the-other-said-ness
Of every day. Nobody knows
What one becomes except the two inside it
Each of whom knows a different

Something, while all night the crickets
Saw each other in half. So it goes
And keeps on while summer
Ends, someone surrenders, or both

Wander off, distracted by all
They have and all they haven't done.

MEMORY

A probability analysis—he
Could have said and I cold-

Shouldered, a definite
Turn of events, and that

Butterfly big
As my head as the blue

Mop of hydrangea sky
Glowing in the shade.

What if nothing happened
Only might have.

Remember what
A perfect summer

It will be, not too hot,
A little rain. I make it all

This way to please
Myself, reality

And its shadow still
Far out there, possible.

RAIN

Learning to trust sense, not

Memory. Is the burner on. Is burn

The right word. Or on. Finally

The first hard rain of fall and

The roof's alive with nerves, humming-

Birds vanishing day by day from the feeder.

This is the world now. On fire. Letting go

One small thing then another.

EQUINOX

Don't care about brightness
Anymore, how or not
Light happens, don't care about
Dark. Why think hours

Fly or the queen ant draggles
Wings across the table, lost. The world
Does what it does, turning
Out life and infinite

Endings creation performs
More ingeniously than starts. Variety,
Count the ways I might
Poof and hiss, some poor let-

Go balloon blowing itself into
Backflip smithereens. So soon.

BROKEN RENGA

What moon high in the day-
Bright sky? Good penny, wide eye
Its own circus, fancy flight

Dreaming spring though blizzard still
Breathes down from the north.

At least you live in a free country
My German friend says
Over beer. Loving the view

Still a luxury. The moon rises.
The world keeps turning into light.

ASLEEP

Find yourself
Somewhere then

No wings, just delts,
An impeccable breaststroke. Built

To stay aloft, the sky
Floats and lifts, blue and dizzy-

Full of itself, clouds motoring by
Spitting sparks and puffs. It was only

Ever about getting up there, and now
It could all backfire, you might come

Down hard or never, might spin
Out of orbit, spiraling

Thrill. Quick. Laugh and fall
Awake. Don't explain the joke.

CANIS LATRANS

At 300 yards I hear a mouse squeak.
At a hundred see you

Blink. Moonless. Through fog
And snow, which I shake off. Hear my

Whoop at your window, deep
Chill beneath your peltlessness. Doors I spirit

Through. Think hard, think back:
We come from the same place every minute

Hauling our bellies onto the present's
Eroding shore. So your bed is warm

And dry. There's no distance I won't
Travel, treading light, placing each foot in

A deer's footprint. If I choose you'll see me
Sashay down your walk, smudging

The corner of your eye, familiar damp
Whiff of something you feel alive

Inside your hollow walls. Hackles
Thrill. Think: did someone touch you?

I LIKE TO WAKE UP

In the dark, work lifting

Light, the work of laying

Night with its snarls and raised hackles

To rest. How quiet I can be. Before

Sunrise, give over.

LUNAR ECLIPSE

Lying in bed your shadow moves. Lying
Thinking your shadow

Flies across the moon's face. Say *time*
To rise. In the dark

Down here in brush and grass
Small bodies pulse. Almost awake. Say

Blink. Naked eye
Watches the moon vanish, but

Your cheap camera made
For talking keeps seeing

A singular shining orb, not
The giving way, showing

A black field. You
Are talking to yourself

Again. *Why won't you*
Settle for your eyes, memory

Failing? *Be a warm*
Body without devices, watching

The lapsed moon darkly
Sail the hills. It's too early to call

Anyone and you've nothing
Going. Ghost ship, shadow

Wolf, self-smudge. *Since before*
You were time you've felt

This way. Close your eyes
Then. I say *Close your eyes.*

HIVE

In the morning my head hums
And wings. Small bodies wriggle

My ears, tidy their chambers. Flesh
Crawling, abuzz, I have

No need for combs but so many
Questions. What on earth

Did I dream, for example, and Where is
Sting. How did they find

Themselves in? Occupied, never
Have I been so gently kept.

HAWK

Be a creature whose one will is life.
Grosbeaks and buntings fuss around the feeder

Of one mind: to eat together and drop
Back into the trees. Be a leaf

Turning under wind, willing
To be shuffled and nosed by bees, no reason

Not to be known. Give over as moose
Does to largeness and smell or

Like the dogs to voice or the continuous
Nuanced alphabet the weasel's long tail

Draws across the grass; lift on evening
Updraft, one eye on the ground, heart

Rising with the body, carried—
Hold the body hard.

HIDEOUT

Two children are hiding in the dark hollow between lilacs, two stolen bone cups tipped over in the dirt, spilling red punch, white lips aglow in the shadows of leaves.

Oh, if their mothers find those cups missing from the whatnot shelf behind polished glass doors, mothers who know nothing on purpose.

Things to be looked at, never touched.

Deep in fragrance and kissing, neither knows what is who.

Laden, spilling over they are their bodies.

Ask me to imagine one body I love. I can't

Call it my own, can't call out the body that is present or gone already though it seems through a trick of time, a sleight of hand, still right here.

SUMMER HAS NO DAY

And so is endless any
Given afternoon, and who can tell

One from the other, the roses heavy,
Bearing their burdens into twilight

And spices lading them, as if thorns
Could make an arch

Architecture, unbreakable. The cane
Does not break, the flower

Does. A shatter on the walk, dark
And bruised. Wasn't it fresh

This morning? Didn't we, on our way to the car,
Stop a moment and breathe its passing?

AUGUST

It is the east, and Juliet. It's rising
Hot and bearing itself in its arms. It is
The longest day, the slowest; for weeks

It goes on forever, a spoon telling seconds
Against the cup's rim and light falling
Full through the window, falling until I can't

Believe how quickly. Then
Shadows growing, days smelling of slow
Burn and sweaters drooping sleeves

Over the edges of drawers. Almost
Time. The crickets can't sleep. They note
Their panic deep into the night.

MATCHLESS

Some organisms change gender

When reproductive opportunity arises.
Snails and hawkweeds can reproduce solely

By parthenogenesis, having nothing else
In common we can see. Some,

Apparently, don't need love at all.
What would you give for such

Independence? Look at this,
Matchless, red stripes blazing. Only,

It will never walk out again.

SHELL

Is it more beautiful now

It is broken? Baroque
Bark frail and wave-

Flung, sharp-struck so exactly

Fractured, softness
Scoured out, each half

Swirling and turning into

Itself, drawing out
Secrets. Mother-of-pearl left

One for each pocket smooth

The palm of each hand. Curved
There. Nestling. Heft

And glimmer its own shape.

VISITING THE DINOSAURS

We are full of air

And time. I never knew

A skull could look so

Horned and socketed,

A kind of lace

Hardened over eons, again

Recuperated. And the spine,

Too, latticed. Imagine

An idea drifting through

An emotion. Long, lifting

Hunger into topmost

Branches, the articulated line.

LANDSCAPE WITH BRONZES
AND LITTLE ROOMS

Down near the garden, art
Bares verdigris teeth, crocodile
Wrestling serpent, the lion laying
Lamb down forever. At bottom,

The rooms are old and intimate, one
Green doorway and vista giving
To another, yew bough and oak and holly
Making walls and ceilings then opening

Grey sky, a deep green lake
Where tame ducks flick their tails.
We hold hands. We know we could lose
Ourselves in here, caught in our dreaming

Like Adam and Eve on the plaza
Outside the café, perfectly stilled, overlooking
Six real gardeners bent to low hedges,
Scissors boxing them right into shape.

DREAM

Outside my friend's window a path

Branches. Down the right fork
He finds an apple tree, twisted and old

As any story, though nothing says

Fairy tale to him. Down the left fork—
But he's never seen the left fork.

The apples are too delicious.

IN THE GARDEN

A turtle with a candle on its back
Lights your way. How slowly you walk

Where the turtle leads—along the path
Or under broad leaves into the undergrowth, asking

What it keeps in its ancient brain. Your mind
Wanders, which holds, you think,

So much. In its shell, it carries a world
Ending; it smells wet earth, a creek running over

There. Its small head cranes, neck bending
Pointedly. Curiosity a kind of grace. Your own.

LANDSCAPE WITH BODIES

It doesn't matter the place is littered with them,
Feeding worms, feeding weeds,

Generations deep, bone
Unhinging from bone, flesh falling

Shred by shred away. Don't bother to think
Who you carry inside you, millennia

Zipping and unzipping, little
Fragments of this and that becoming

A speck of green in your eye, the way
Your neck turns. All those deaths

Planted in your cells, cartoon bombs crazy-
Wired to clocks, and you can't know which

Will blast off first until
Too late. Better point to a boneyard

Oak digging roots in, flipping
Breezy leaves, insouciant: *Now*

You see me. We know
Rocks are indifferent, but we carve them

Pithy sayings, *If a body need*
A body, etc., as if spelling could

Return us, sensible as ever.

AWAY

There are reasons for wanting distance.

The impulse may begin with a blade of grass or the brash sweep of goose-honk over the ear. But how did it carry you here? No tree, no well or pasture, no moss soft for your step. Only ice and stone shifting underfoot, opening and closing. Only sky and stars, present or absent, cold either way.

Sometimes you know you could die of anything, and you do not shiver. Having been borne across deserts, through forests, over mountains and water to be here, you are light and strong as a gust of wind.

Somewhere, an engineer is imagining a sail, an engine, ways to give you wings. Press a key: escape.

Here the eye pinpoints and the birds are eccentric and personable.

Not a legless beast nor microscopic lichen belongs to the home you've left; not an ear recognizes your voice above the wind, and you still love everything, bedazzled.

Who says this isn't the world.

You have not withdrawn. You have plunged in deep.

Who can say what will call the heart, or fill it.

∞

away

there are reasons for **wanting** distance.

the impulse may begin with a blade of grass or the brash
sweep of goose-honk over the ear. but how did it carry
you here? no tree, no well or pasture, no moss soft for
your step. only ice and stone shifting underfoot, opening
and closing. only **sky and stars**, present or absent, cold
either way.

sometimes **you** know you could die of anything, and you
do not **shiver**. having been borne across deserts, through
forests, over mountains and water to be here, **you** are
light and strong as a **gust** of wind.

somewhere, an engineer is imagining a sail, an engine
new ways to give you wings. press a key: **escape**.

                    how we sing

                    the lion's throat, in stitches. **riding**
                    the backs of dragons. bohemian,

                    spare-pantried, squeezing our boxes,
                    penises wagging, breasts akimbo, mouthing

                    feet, hearts in our hands, whistles
                    whetted. **bare** faced. captive. in **time**.

NOTES

Page 17: Written in response to Maureen O'Hara Ure's painting by the same title.

Page 20: "The Archimedes Palimpsest" is a manipulated erasure of Edward Rothstein's "Finding Archimedes in the Shadows," *New York Times*, October 17, 2011.

Page 28: All the language in this poem is lifted, mostly in full sentences, from "The Life of Pi and Other Infinities" by Natalie Angier; "In a Place for the Dead, Studying a Seemingly Immortal Species" by Hillary Rosner; and "Study Suggests Lower Death Rate for the Overweight," by Pam Belluck, all of which appeared in the *New York Times* on December 31, 2012 and January 1, 2013.

Page 33: After hearing a talk on the IMPACT Mummy Database.

Page 34: The italicized lines are from the *Song of Solomon* and the Wikipedia entry on terminal dehydration.

Page 39: For Helen Louise Fullman.

Page 46: The critic is Guy Davenport, taking about Ronald Johnson.

Page 47: The italics in the first line are Morris's. The other italicized lines are sentences Morris quotes in the original *New York Times* Opinionator Blog, "What's in a Name (Part 3)," published May 3, 2012. These lines, respectively, are from Magritte, *Austral English and OED*, Sojourner Truth, and Captain Cook. The "typo" is mine.

Page 48: Psalm 104, For Lincoln Ure.

Page 50: For Isaac Newton. Italicized quote is Newton quoting Barrow about poetry.

Page 55: For Catie Crabtree, who introduced me to the idea that the mango is a bedroom fruit, with which she disagrees.

Page 56: As he left his trial for heresy, where in exchange for his life he denied that the earth orbits the sun, Galileo is said to have whispered, "And yet it does move."

Page 58: For my father.

Page 65: After May Swenson.

Page 72. Winston Churchill called depression "the black dog." With thanks to Maureen O'Hara Ure.

Page 74: The British Museum, Ice Age Art: arrival of the modern mind, April 2013. Italicized lines are from the exhibit commentary. The aurochs is among the animals represented on the walls of Lascaux; the last recorded aurochs died in Poland's Jaktorów Forest in 1627.

Page 80: Titled with a line from Robert Kirshner, the *New York Times*.

Page 84: For Melanie Rae Thon.

Page 86: The poem was written for and is here "broken" out of *The World Keeps Turning to Light: A Renga by the State Poets Laureate of America.*

Page 94: For Kathryn Stockton.

Page 95: Title from *The Other Side of Paradise.*

Page 99: Natural History Museum of Utah.

Page 100: Botanical Garden of Brussels.

Page 101: For Wyn Cooper.

Pages 43, 76, 106: The infinity erasures are for Melanie Rae Thon.

BIOGRAPHICAL NOTE

Katharine Coles's memoir, *Look Both Ways*, was published in 2018. She is a Poet-in-Residence at the Natural History Museum of Utah and the SLC Public Library for the Poets House program FIELD WORK, and was sent to Antarctica in 2010 to write poems under the auspices of the National Science Foundation's Antarctic Artists and Writers Program (*The Earth Is Not Flat*, Red Hen Press 2012). She has received grants from the NEA and NEH and a 2012 Guggenheim Fellowship.

www.ingramcontent.com/pod-product-compliance
Lightning Source LLC
Chambersburg PA
CBHW021507090426
42739CB00007B/512